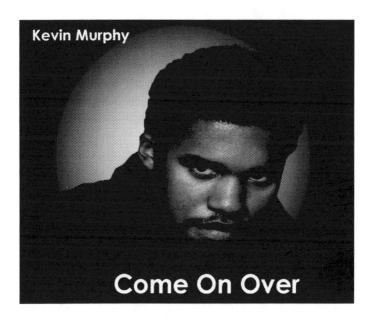

Kevin Murphy

Come On Over

Come On Over

Kevin Murphy

authorHOUSE®

AuthorHouse™
1663 Liberty Drive
Bloomington, IN 47403
www.authorhouse.com
Phone: 1-800-839-8640

First published by AuthorHouse   10/17/2011

ISBN: 978-1-4670-6095-0 (sc)
ISBN: 978-1-4670-6096-7 (ebk)

Library of Congress Control Number: 2011918189

Printed in the United States of America

Contents

Follow Me

Ups and downs I go through
I am not perfect
There and back
I go on, a never-ending story
Situations arise
Reality's covered ground, baby
Fantasy and dreams aside
I am not perfect

I come from afar
But I mean no trouble
I go by a plan, a pattern
Finishing unfinished business
Take my hand
Because when I dream
You're part of it all
Follow me.

Over and over again
I struggle to meet ends
So I can rest—in time
But I am a fool to believe
I can conclude my life's journey
It won't stop until I die
So why do I continue to act
Like an old soul trapped in
A little boy's body?

Questions come to mind
Many left unanswered
The way things are, I can't
And I don't mean to tell a soul
Because I don't know why
We live like we do
I just follow along, moving on

Through thick and thin
Count me in the game
Take my hand
And never let it go
When circumstances hit bottom
Don't oppose me
Follow me.

I don't know what will
Happen to me, to you
But we'll see—one way or another

Talk

Though you speak little
Your body tells me much
The words are there
Unspoken

Lucky for me to understand
What move to make
What words to say
But often, your body language
Can be misleading
Do not leave me guessing

In time, there will be disagreements
(I hate to think about it)
Do not think I'd ignore you
I care about every word you say
That leads me to understand
Where we are in this love affair

Open your heart to me
As you would your arms
I need to know how much you need me
If you were to take it there
It would all be simple
We can take ourselves
And take this to the next level

But before we move on
I have to know
How do you feel in words than
The language of your body

If You Dare
(In This Love Affair)

Open your eyes
And smile for me
If you dare
Look me up like you
Never done
Come about
If you dare

In this love affair
Intimidation leads me
I don't have the bravery
So I keep still
Hoping you'll catch on
Then understand me

Wrap your arms around mine
Whisper in my ears
If you dare
Let me show you
My true feelings for you
If you dare

We have no need
To be dead in this love affair

Honestly

Qualities I possess
You know how I am
I think it funny
When you think of me otherwise
I can be lousy
Even rude
But you see me
At my best today
Smiling

Holding my hand
I'm catching your eyes
Picking up some clues
My detective

Sometimes
I can't find the words
At the moment
I would take a rain check
"Ask me later"
I tell you
But I never answer

I'd rather for you not to
Know every detail of me
Until further notice
When I feel it's all right
To come true of the things
You have not discovered

Your bitter demands
Curling your lips
Please stop

I need time
Sincerely
And if you do understand
I do love you
I just need time

Baby

Your body is somethin' else
One of the finest creations ever
Your eyes, your lips
Your breast, your hips
Got me wanting to take you
To a room
But making love to you
Don't amount to anything
If you're not as sweet
As you are now, baby

Your sex drive is a plane
Ticket to Hawaii
The ride's exciting as the trip
You are a work of art
When you want to be
Got the other girls
Tailing behind
Dying to know your secret
And why I just can't be
With them, baby

Your mind is extraordinary
If I take the time
I can easily see why
You're all I need
To get on with my life
So all I want to do is

8

Thank you, care for you
Love you
And I got to say that's
Worth more than you can
Ever imagine, baby

For You

For you, I believed
For you, I loved
For you, I struggled to have ends meet
I never let my guard down for you
Because I loved you

There and back
Without question
I sacrificed everything to be with you
I devoted my time and effort
To learn to love you
Even though people around us
Thought I was crazy
But I thought I saw a different side of you

If I did all of that for you
The least you can do
Is not blind me from the truth
Show me how you care

For you, I made promises
For you, I broke them
For you, I catered—

To every whine, whim, and whisper
I was determined to build on this love
Make it last
And satisfy your every wish
Just for and only you

If I did all of that for nothing
You were a waste of time

Let Go

Well, well, well
Your bonus points been used
One day, I held on
And then I had to let you go

If I have given the green light
To spend the remainder of my
Days with you
I am deeply sorry
If I told you, promised you
Promises a dozen
I regret of breaking them
But you left me no choice

I was easily influenced
Subjected under your wing
I was powerless
You did one hell of a job
Befriended me, played me
Cutting my legs
I didn't get respect
Just a stab in the back
Robbing me from my good
Where I couldn't see it

You son of a gun!
You thought you were something
Knocking me down
Until the bruises got deep
You fool!
You thought you could
Keep me from rising
This game you created has
Failed success
You lose. I win

Never Comin' Back

I don't know why you
Keep talking to me
Tracking me down
Following my shadow
I can't trust to go on
Without you tailing behind
What is it that you want?

My friends tell me you
Want to start over with me
If it is so, I'm sorry that
I can't trust another try
You made your bed
So now you have to lie in it

I heard you've got someone else
I hope he's worth it
Don't think you're going to
Win me over through jealousy

The nights I lied awake
Thinking you could do better
Than treat me as a doormat
Are gone out the window
You warmed out your welcome
Before I changed the locks

All access is denied.

Focus (Come On Over)

Walking distances
I am ahead
You are behind
Spaces between
I ease off the gas
Hope you'll catch up
It's takin' you forever
I'm losing patience

I sent you a message
Come on over
Talk to me
Eat. Drink
Make yourself comfortable
I'm only human
I don't bite

When I get the nerve
To speak to you
Listen. Look me
In the eye
If you dedicate time
Read between the lines
You will discover
I can be an open book
Get to know me

I don't ask much
Just want your respect
Trust me
I have my reasons
And I can be a good friend
You will find the rumors
To be untrue
But I must warn you
You better stop with
That foolish talk about me
It's a funny way to
Show your gratitude

Silly Gossip

Let's go for a walk
Somewhere quiet
Get to know me better
Put me on the stand
Express what's on your mind
Ask questions
Don't hold in

Step into my office
Pull up a seat
Rest your body
I want you to give it to me
Throw at me. I'm ready

You heard the silly talk
What do you believe?
Do you even care as you
Sit in their company
Snickering at the mention
Of my name?

Those drama kings!
When I turn my back
They're pointing at me
I feel their eyes watching me
Looking for an expression
To please their satisfaction
But guess what?
It doesn't phase me at all

They say I'm just an easy target
The one they can take advantage
Of and leave me hurting
But they don't know me
Or what I'm capable of

Here

Here you go, opening the door
Stepping inside, coming thru
Think you're so cool, huh?

We're all looking at you
Because as far as we know
There is only one clown
In this place—and it's you

There you go, talking the
Trash you talk, throwing things
Against the wall
Think you're so bad, huh?

We are not amused because
We know that you aren't
Fooling anyone—but yourself

Welcome to this place!
Don't have to make a grand
Appearance because nobody
Is better than other

Here we summon to have
A good time, be children at fun
Talk and listen; laugh and cry
Share stories and dine over
The food laid before us

Be yourself
That's all you have to be
And we'll love you

Throw away all the negativity
Hatred has no meaning here

This Place

I am not ashamed to
Tell you a place I
Know so well. Listen

This place excels every
Place I have ever been
Because in this place
I would rather be

Through these doors
There lies a history
In this place.
A story is told
In this place.

Anybody who's anybody
May come to this place
No limitations.
We got all you need
Come sup with us
In this place

Come on over!

Be

I don't care what they
Think about me
I don't care what they
Say about me
Because it doesn't matter
What they think
And it doesn't matter
What they say
I can only be me

It makes no difference
How they feel about me
It makes no difference
What they see in me
'Cause I don't need somebody
To watch my every move
And tell me what I need
Or need not to do
I can only be me

The way I live is my
Own decision
I don't need instructions
Respect that and
Stay out of my business

What you expect of me
It's impossible to follow
But I cannot live up to
Your expectations
What you ask of me
I cannot achieve the rules
The only thing I can be
More anything
Is myself, and that's all

Square

The room's gettin' small
And smaller . . .
And smaller . . .
And smaller . . .
The walls cave in
As the ceiling moves down
The doors are locked
The windows are sealed
I cannot get out

The room's gettin' dark
And darker . . .
And darker . . .
And darker . . .
I am scared
Though I try to scream
Nobody hears my voice
I cannot get out

The air I lose
I cannot breathe
Panicking, trembling
Sweating
A mess all over
Running into dead ends
Bumping heads with concrete
I cannot breathe
I cannot get out

Rescue me

Open The Door

Little boy
Who are you foolin'?
Look at you
You're an animal
Nobody wants to come your way
It's easy to see why

On days so fine
You spend the time
Watching the sun set in the West
Shaking your head
Regretting the time you spent
Doing absolutely nothing

How does it feel to dig
Your own grave at a very young age?
How does it feel to give up, give in
When deep inside, you want out?

Little boy
You've got much to learn
Life is too short
Ain't much time
Better get up, get out, give in
Because every breath, every heartbeat
Has an end
Then it's over

Do not drop the anchor here
Sail your ships, little sailor
Live your life
Open the door

Room 4 More

He shot an arrow
Into the night's sky
Made a move
Got a voice
Established his own freedom
Destiny fulfilled
In all of his getting
He's blessed
Every time
And whatever he receives
He calls it his own
But wait
There's always room for more

He respects
He admires the independent ones
That's him
Down-to-earth
Being nobody else
That's him
And, frankly
He's satisfied with the things he's got
Though, wait
There's room for more

He can do without
The heavy stuff
It's the simple things
He's looking for
And there's always room for more

Make Over

Flashbacks of coming along
I was alone, feeling lonely
Done with what's-her-name
Life moves on

Then came you
Met you in the club
As if the potter saw fit
At first, I was scared
Didn't want another breakup
But I couldn't resist the tempts
As I saw you dancing on the floor

Look at what we have here
A glamorous body going
To and fro, off and on
Around and around
Snapping your fingers
Getting funky to the groove
With your eyes on me
Never saw a woman more beautiful

I'm wishing to take you home
Obviously, you got feelings
For me, and I don't want to be alone
Life moves on
I ain't gonna miss a beat, another
Opportunity for love
with a taste of you, I'm living in joy

That's what I'm talking about
You're feeling me
I'm feeling you. No regrets

Blue Jeans

She could do with a fur vest
Or a funky dress
But she chose her blue jeans
Among the clothes in her
Closet

Sexy. Really, really sexy
Dabbed in perfume
Scent pleasing to taste
Damn

Her style is simple, plain:
A white t-shirt riding her
Breasts
A pair of blue jeans
Hiding the rest of her goods

Blue jeans, they got it made
Fastened to her bottom
Taking up the space
Somewhere I just can't get
(I'm jealous)

Interlude

Sexambition (sek am bish'n) N.—

1. A strong desire to have sex.
2. The act that one desires sex so strongly.
3. Sexual desire.

Sexambition

All day, all night
I think about sex

Early mornin'
Woke up with a start
Not by the sound of the alarm
But the cravin' in my heart
Then I knew
The tides in my ocean
Rose to their highest peak
Hormones at bay
Ecstasy washin' all over me
Feelin' uneasy, feelin' crazy
Was 'bout to explode
Where was my safety?

Paid a visit to the phone
Had you on speed dial
Under the impression it
Was safe to call
Than walk a quarter of a mile
But when I picked up the receiver
I froze so suddenly
Feelin' selfish
Feelin' inconsiderate
Wondering were you feelin' me

Now I got to keep my cool
For respect isn't just a word
If I'm only in this myself
It would be absurd
To make love to you
With you playing pretend
We can do this together
But are you in?

Want to fulfill your fantasy
Give you a good time
Make you feel good
Blow your mind
What're the plans?
Set demands
Make, schedule appointments
I'd be your schoolboy
But don't wait too long
'Cause I think about you
All day, all night
Can I come on over?
We'll take it slower and slower
Light candles, play jazz music
Make love over and over

Baby, feel free to
Give me a ring
Baby, let me know
When you're ready

And Then She Says

Got off work
Ain't tired
Been up all day
Soar. Energetic
Walking home

Got my cell phone
At hand, ready
To receive a call from
My lady
I'm just waiting for
The signal

Then I get a beep
And it's her
I pick up suddenly
"What's goin' on?"
Then she goes
"Nothin' much, baby"

And then she says
"Come on over
I need you to
Come on over
It's you
And it's you alone who
Could make me
Feel so good inside"

I say, "Yes"

Turn Off the Light

If I could blind you
From sight
I'll do it tonight
Lend your sight to the
Sensational Ray Charles
If he was alive

Now before you get
Comfortable, strip me
From my clothes
Help me fulfill my
Fantasy
Turn off the light

Queen, tonight is yours
I'm here to make your
Dreams come true, too
But we'll do well
If you wouldn't mind
Flipping that switch

Put your trust in me
You have my word
I can offer more than
You ask
Until you want nothing more
It's a package deal
But I won't do well
With the light switch on

I won't bite
I promise.

A Physical Thing

We set this thing out
You and me
Got ourselves a room
Cheap price, $30.00
Laughing, giggling
Sex on the mind

When we make love
You're aware of what you're in for
'Cause when we make love
We don't fall in love
This is just a physical thing

You're there for me
I'm there for you
Whatever you want, I got
Whatever you need, I have
See nothin' wrong with
Satisfying our needs
No strings attached

It's easy to slip
Cross the border
Fall in love, I mean
Emotions pull through, I feel
You feel it too
Don't take it personal
Don't in love

Don't fall in love with me
Ain't the time now
No, no, no, no, no
Build your walls on concrete ground
And I'll build mine
But, baby, have no tears
'Cause I feel a vibe
And it's telling me so
This could be, someday—*love*

Heartbreaker

Until now, I've kissed many lips
I've signed OFF on various relationships
After I got what I wanted
I called it QUITS
Cashed out, signed off
Then fled the scene
As if the day never occurred

Upon my account, I am
Responsible for the broken
Hearts I have broken
Just as they settled in
I was packing my bags
Heading off to play someone else
Didn't bother to give a reason

They cursed me
They called me names
They threatened me never
To return again
I was a thief in the night
'Cause I've stolen more than
I've brought before I met them

The road's getting dense
Watch out!
WARNING posters of me over town
Everybody's on the look out
Better watch my step. Got to
Do it quick

Angel in disguise
Have got your arms around my neck
You want to claim me
It's too bad you didn't check
My references
I've got your heart in my hand
Only a matter of time before
I break it

I did it once
I can do it again

Secrets

Better watch what you say to me
Be careful of the words you say
We might be heard next door
So, chose your words carefully

The secrets you tell to me
It is you against everyone
When you tell me your secrets
I'm involved by voicing my opinion

These private talks we hold
Makes this friendship stronger
But outside this matter
I'm losing the people we talk about

Going around their backs
We think we are smart
You may think they don't
Know what we're talking about
But they know everything
How can we keep these
Secrets long?
We have got to stop this
Before we lose the people
We talk about

This is childish! We are men
I don't want to take sides
Sick and tired of being the
Pages in your diary
Have got to stop these secrets

Who?

Who died
And made you boss?

Fight Call

Come and finish it
You can't just end
What you already started

Out the box, made apparent
You got hate
Fight it off, hit me
I called you a name
Don't just stand there
Do somethin'

There is no turnin' back
Better come and finish it

I got a plan: step up
Throw the first punch
Then we're on
C'mon, don't be scared
You got a reputation
So keep it

Come and finish it
You can't just end
What you started
There is no turning back
Better come and finish it

I don't care who you bring
And I don't care what they say
Let me get mine
Get yours
Come and finish it

Control

They call you Thunder 'cause
Your actions are intimidating
They cater to your every need
They are slaves to your world
They call you King
But if they look the right way
You are nothing, just a guy
Trying to be in control
And that's alright
You've got great intentions
But no brains 'cause to think
I would call you King and
Cater to your every need
You must be insane

See, I am not the one to fall as victim
I am not anyone's prey
So you say what you have to say
To me, your words have no meaning

I've come too fat to let it all go down
Give this up and crown somebody King

They say to oppose you is bad
For my health
Well, I feel no illness
So now you have word that
I won't bow to you

It feels like a crime
I heard you're going after me
And won't stop 'til you reach the finish line
Oooh, aaah. Bring it on

I've come too far to lose it all
Lose myself and give my all
To somebody called King

I was raised with high morals
I was raised to respect myself
Not to be as used clothing
Or a toy on yourself
It's like that
Failure is not an option of mine
If you want a fight, come and get it
Let's set this right, and when we're finished
I don't want any hard feelings
Just to let you know who you're dealing
with

I am King. I am in control
I don't take anybody's orders but my own
So, I'm not, and I won't be a slave
To cater to your every need

Freedom

Beyond reach, out of bounds
Out of sight, in peace
In control, powerful
Cool, calm, collected
Untreated, unaffected

Feel the words I feel
As I close my eyes, then breathe

Feel the air being inhaled
In and out of my lungs
And the silence melts to the
Sound of my heart beating
(That's how I know I'm alive)

While the fire dies
And the room grows cold
Less activity coming from
Me goes on
But I am not asleep
Thinking freely about my life
(That's how brilliant ideas are born)

Undisturbed, disconnected
The cell phone is put on SILENT
Incoming calls, I am not worried
They'll just have to wait
Same for the visitors outside
This door with a sign labeled
"PLEASE DON'T DISTURB!"

They'll just have to wait
Another day
This is my time now
And when I venture out
See me, going on, moving forward
Beginning and finishing
Taking in, rejecting projects
At my own pace, in demand

To be free, to feel free, to realize
You're free . . . that's freedom

Don't

These cuts and scars you left
Will always remain to be seen
Still, I'm holding unto the good
Times you put me through

Since it is over
And my freedom rings
I won't lose myself
And tell everybody what
You're all about

Do not think I'd make you
Out to be the enemy
Do not expect your name
To be in the headlines
Because of me
I'm better than that

Do not be scared when
I come by your way
Do not fear when I see
You with others
Don't worry. Your secret
Is safe with me

It is not my duty to tell
What you're all about
It is for them to find out
For themselves

No, I won't make a scene
No, I won't bring you down
That is not my victory

Homeboy

Without you, the puzzle is undone
I cannot picture myself moving on
Reaching new heights and challenges
In my life without your company
Without you, I'm incomplete

My life has changed since you'd
Stepped into my world
My days are nothing short
But fun and games
Because of you, I'm smiling
All the way
(Man! I feel my cheek muscles aching!)

You might think all the things
You say and do
Don't mean much
But they do

For it was you who answered my
Calling when no one bothered to care
For it was you who gave me a
Shoulder to lean upon when I was
A boat in troubled water
It was you who brought me company
When I felt lonely
It was you who fought my battles
When I felt numb

You might think I'm blind
To realize all you've done
But I see clearly behind these eyes
Of all the things you've done
You didn't have to
But I'm proud you did

If there's anything you need
Never fear to ask me
For you, I'll do anything
You got it

It's you and me 'til the end

Girl

My boy told me you'd be
Around for a long time
I began to notice that his
Word proved to be true
It seems to me that you
Two could hit it off well
He's been hitting me up
Giving me the daily news

It wouldn't surprise me
If he pops the question
I have known him for too
Long to give up so easily
Since he met you, I am the
Second best in his world
But you know, he makes
It feel like the old days

With you, he spends time
Loving you in and out
And when we see each other
It's magical! We pick up
Where we left off
Catching up on old times
Being the best of friends
It hurts when we depart

He was my best friend
He was my brother
There're days I wish things
Could stay the way they were
But when I look at you two
I let go gracefully
Because I realize my time
With him was done

Look after him
Take care of him for me

Ride

Child? I ain't no child
The one who spends his days
Within these dark walls.
I'm a bird, waiting on you
To use the key
The anticipation rides in me
Waiting on you to unbolt the lock
So, open the door, and let's go

Dress to your best
Yeah, do that thing
As I sit on the bed
Making plans, daydreaming about
Our little night's adventure
The night is young

HA! You could be my taxi driver
"All aboard!"
I could be your passenger
Drive me to our destination
I love it better when we
Go by style in your funky car

I just want to get out
Roll down the window, please
Want to feel the night's cool
Breeze brush against my skin
Oh, don't make a hurry
Want to stick my head out
And enjoy the ride

As we ride, the city lights go blur
All that's around me is silent
Except the sound of the motor
I'm free! I'm free! I'm free!
Then I hear your voice
We're here at our destination

Women

They are the icing on the cake
They got their fingers twisted
Around the strings of men's hearts
Women.

They are the winners in the game
They follow the rules
Yet the men cannot understand
They cannot keep up
Women.

They put the "brave" in bravery
They'll stand their ground
For their men
Absolutely.

They do not forget
Every little thing you do
To put that gleam in their eyes
When all they wanted was
Your time
Women.

They're tops to the jars
If you want a cookie inside
Best show them respect
Be good to them
And they would to you

I tip my hat to them
Because they're worth forevermore
Your pocket values
I know
Women.

You can visit me at
www.mrkevinmurphy.com.

Check back often
to find the latest news!